MOVING HOME

Essential Guide

Glynis Kozma

First published in Great Britain in 2010 by
Need2Know
Remus House
Coltsfoot Drive
Peterborough
PE2 9JX
Telephone 01733 898103
Fax 01733 313524
www.need2knowbooks.co.uk
Need2Know is an imprint of Forward Press Ltd.
www.forwardpress.co.uk
All Rights Reserved
© Glynis Kozma 2010
SB ISBN 978-1-86144-085-3
Cover photograph: Stockxpert

Contents

Introduction

Congratulations! Whether you're leaving for university, or about to buy or rent your first home, this is one of the most exciting stages in life.

Leaving home is a rite of passage – you might do it very successfully, like a proverbial duck to water, or it can be a rude awakening. This book will make the transition as smooth as possible, so you can enjoy every minute of the process.

According to UCAS, in 2009 there were 477,277 new students going to university. However, students do drop out of university, with significant numbers doing so in the first year. So why do students drop out? Sometimes it's because the course they have chosen isn't right for them, others do so for more personal reasons or because they cannot cope with being independent.

For some people, cooking can present a problem – but sometimes other factors can come into play, like disorganisation, poor budgeting or lack of inspiration. In the longer term, this can cause more serious problems with your money and your health. Homesickness or relationships can be also difficult to deal with on top of the new responsibilities associated with leaving home.

No matter how independent you want to be, the reality of living on your own can be tricky at times. It can be disheartening to discover that life away from the family is not as easy as was perhaps imagined. It can also be difficult to admit you are struggling, and you might not know where to get help. With the expectation that you can now fend for yourself, you might feel anxious about asking your parents for advice and support.

However, with a bit of planning and organisation, making the transition from home to university, and/or to living independently, can be easy – and really fun!

This book gives clear and wide-ranging advice on the following 'essential' areas:

- Choosing a flat or house.
- Personal safety.

- Cooking.

- Budgeting.

- Household chores.

- Laundry.

- Personal relationships.

- Emotional and physical health.

Thousands of young people leave home and love their independence. This guide shows you how to overcome as well as prevent any possible problems, so enjoy reading it, and have fun with your new found freedom.

Disclaimer

This book is for general information on the issues that surround leaving home for the first time. Any medical information contained within the book should not be used to replace professional medical advice. Always seek professional medical advice from your GP!

Chapter One

Your Finances

Let's start with the most important factor in leaving home – money. To be completely responsible for your income and your home can be quite daunting, but with some planning you can avoid many of the common pitfalls. Depending on whether you have had a regular income previously, you may know how to manage your incoming money and your outgoings. If not, then this is the time to learn. If you are a student, you probably have a student loan, topped up with any earnings from part-time work or support from your parents.

First, a bank account is essential and most people have one already. There are so many to choose from, so it's good to shop around – don't necessarily stick with what you have as there may be better deals. Check the charges, if there are any, because you will probably be using more banking facilities, such as direct debits and standing orders, than you have before. Many banks have inviting offers for students and young people, but read the small print carefully. The overdraft limits can vary, as do the interest charges.

You should be realistic about your income:

- Your net income is the amount you will live on, so ensure you know your weekly or monthly income after tax and deductions.

- If you are a student, you will most likely have a student loan, plus any earnings of your own, or contributions from your family.

- Do not include bonuses or any other income unless it is guaranteed; being optimistic about what you might be paid will not pay the bills. If you know for certain that your loan or salary will rise each year, or that promotion is guaranteed, then take this into account, but be realistic.

- If you do work that is seasonal or very occasional, you should look on those earnings as a bonus for non-essentials – do not factor this into your essential outgoings.

'Many banks have inviting offers for students and young people, but read the small print carefully. The overdraft limits can vary, as do the interest charges.'

How much can you afford?

A rough rule-of-thumb is one-third of your net income for rent or mortgage. So, if your net monthly income is £900, you could allow up to £300 for accommodation. This obviously varies depending on your other commitments, such as transport costs and any other payments you make from your bank account regularly.

In order to know how much you can afford, you need to establish your essential outgoings. Once you know these, you can then look at properties, either to rent or buy, and establish what is within your budget. At one end of the scale will be a house or flat you could afford to buy, followed by renting on your own, then sharing a house or flat. The cheapest option of all will be a bedsit or lodgings (a room in a house owned by someone else).

Student accommodation

If you are a student, you will most probably have a student loan; how much this is will depend on your family circumstances. It will pay for your accommodation or living expenses, but probably not both. One of these will either be funded by your parents or you if you take some part-time work during term time, or full-time temporary work during holidays.

If you can choose your student accommodation in your first year – which is usually in halls – have a look at the options as costs vary. Take into consideration not only the cost but the location and any extra expenses such as fares. Your only additional costs are possibly a telephone in your room (it's worth finding out if this is cheaper than your mobile if you have one) and/or an Internet connection. The student accommodation office will be able to provide you with a price list, so you can look at costs before making any decisions.

One of your main considerations should be whether to choose catered or self-catered halls. Catered means you are provided with breakfast and an evening meal, self-catered means you have facilities to cook for yourself, sharing a kitchen with a group of other students. Catered halls are more expensive, but this option might suit you if you don't like cooking. The downside is that although you will always have a choice of meals, you won't have as much choice as if you cook for yourself. If you self-cater, you will be responsible for all your own shopping, budgeting and cooking. However, this can be the cheaper option as you only buy what you need, whereas in catered halls you pay for all of your meals even if you aren't there for them – which could become frustrating!

If you are a student who is not living in halls, but you have to find your own accommodation, then all the following information about choosing a house or flat will be relevant.

Deposits

Whether you are buying or renting, you will need a deposit. This could be anything from 10% possibly up to 25% of the purchase cost, depending on whom your mortgage is with. You will have to show that you have this deposit before you obtain your mortgage.

If you rent, you will need a deposit of one month's rent or more, and usually a month's rent in advance as well. When you rent, the deposit is returnable, with deductions for any damage. You will find that many agents charge you a fee for finding the flat or house, so make sure you are aware of this before you commit to renting the property. There may also be a fee for running a credit check – these fees are around £30-40, so be wary if agents want to charge a lot more than this.

Essential monthly outgoings

- Utility bills – gas and/or electric, water, telephone/Internet connection. If you are moving into university halls, you won't have to pay bills but just an accommodation fee.

- Insurance – contents insurance and/or buildings insurance.

- Council tax – this may not apply to you if you share a house or are a full-time student.

- TV licence – this can be paid monthly or annually.

- Transport – fares and/or fuel, road tax and insurance, savings for ongoing repairs and MOTs.

- Food.

- Repayment of loans – student loan, car loan or any other debts you may have (you won't need to pay your student loan back until you enter employment).

- Clothes – you won't buy clothes every month, but you might want to save a small amount each month towards essential clothes that you will buy a few times a year.

Your non-essential outgoings will include entertainment, holidays, CDs and books – any kind of leisure or lifestyle expenditure could be considered non-essential.

You should be able to calculate how much you can afford for rent or a mortgage this way. If you are unsure how much your utility bills will be, ask the current occupant if you intend to house share or rent, or ask friends how much they pay. There will usually be a standing charge each month or quarter, on top of the amount you use.

Budgeting for utility bills

When you move in, you should supply meter readings for gas and/or electricity to the relevant companies so you do not get charged for the previous occupants' usage.

Your gas and electricity bills will usually arrive every month or quarter and most companies allow you to choose your payment method. You can pay a set amount each month, based on an estimate of how much you will use over the year. If you use less, you will be in credit the following year or you can have your payments adjusted. If you use more, then you will have to top-up your monthly payment.

Alternatively, you could choose to pay quarterly and provide a meter reading to the company each quarter. They can then accurately calculate your bill and only charge you for what you have used; many companies allow you to use a secure login to submit a meter reading to their website. However, choosing this payment method does mean that you will be paying out large sums each quarter, rather than a smaller, more manageable amount each month.

It can be hard to predict what your bills are likely to be. Obviously, how much you use is under your control, but a large flat or house will take more energy to heat than a small flat.

Save on your bills

Here are some tips on how to save energy in your home. This will save you money and should be encouraged as part of a 'greener' household.

- Turn your heating thermostat down by a couple of degrees.
- Use the timer for your heating so it's on for a minimum amount of time each day.
- Turn the lights off when you're not in the room.
- Set your laptop to standby mode, rather than leaving it on when you're not using it.
- Don't use your oven for one dish if you can cook two and freeze one.
- Make up a full load for the washing machine rather than wasting energy on half-full washes.
- Wash on a low heat setting – 30° should be okay for most washes.
- Only tumble dry if you have to.
- Use insulating tape to exclude drafts around windows.
- Check that your loft is insulated – if it isn't and you are a homeowner, you could be eligible for a grant from your council.
- Close the curtains at dusk to help keep the heat in.

If you are going to share your home, then the bills will be divided amongst everyone. However, you may have to convince extravagant users to be more economical!

Paying your bills

Keeping track of your finances is vital to avoid getting into debt. You can make use of technology and establish automatic payments for regular bills. Direct debits and standing orders can easily be organised at your bank, online or by signing an agreement sent to you by the company requesting the payment.

- Direct debit – you instruct the bank to pay the company an amount each month or quarter. This amount does not have to be fixed each month.

- Standing order – you instruct the bank to pay the company a fixed amount each month or quarter.

- Bank transfer – you can do this youself with online banking.

It is much simpler to use these methods of payment for outgoings like council tax, credit card payments, utility bills and other bills that are regular. It means you don't have to remember each month. The only problem is if you want to stop payments – you might have to notify your bank up to a month in advance of the payment date, or you could find the payment cannot be stopped in time.

Paying bills on time can save you money. Some companies apply a penalty for late payment, others offer a small discount if you pay promptly. All credit card companies and other sources of credit will apply interest charges for late or insufficient payment. These charges can be very high, so try to avoid them as much as possible.

When you arrange your direct debits or standing orders, think about when your wages are paid into your account and arrange them so that you know funds will be available when the money is due to go out. For example, do not arrange for all your debits to be paid on the last day of a month if your wages are paid on the first day of each month, or you might find yourself overdrawn.

'Keeping track of your finances is vital to avoid getting into debt. You can make use of technology and establish automatic payments for regular bills.'

The kitty – for house sharers

If you are going to share your home, it is a good idea to have a 'kitty' for essentials such as loo roll, washing-up liquid, household cleaners and maybe even tea, coffee and milk if this is used communally.

If everyone contributes a small sum weekly, such as £5, you can then take it in turns to buy what is needed when you do your own shopping. This saves the hassle of one person always buying, then trying to extract what is owed form everyone else. Receipts can go in the kitty so everyone knows what was bought and when.

Buying on credit

Credit can be useful if you want to buy essentials, such as a washing machine, and have no savings. However, if you can, avoid buying on credit, unless interest-free credit is offered.

If you use a credit card, try to repay the total due each month to avoid high interest charges. Credit schemes usually mean you will pay much more in the long run. It is better to try to save for what you want, if it's a non-essential, or repay any credit as soon as you can.

Store cards

Major retailers offer their own store cards allowing you to buy on credit, and often you can also earn points or discounts with a store card. The disadvantage of store cards is that they present you with another account to manage and it can be easy to overlook the payments due and incur high rates of interest.

Some stores do offer attractive schemes where you can buy monthly with no extra cost, so if you are buying an essential item, such as a washing machine, look at what is on offer.

Overall, it is probably better to stick to just one credit card if you need one, rather than several store cards, as it is so easy to forget to pay each month, or to overspend and end up with large debts. If you're a student, don't forget that you'll get student discount in most highstreet shops – your student union will tell you more, or you can visit www.nus.org.uk for information.

Loyalty cards

A loyalty card is different from a store card. Each time you make a purchase from a particular shop, you log points onto your card which can then be spent in store at a later date. It can be good to save points on your loyalty card throughout the year and use them at Christmas, for example.

Savings

No matter how tight your budget is, always try to save something. Even if you can only manage £10 or £20 a month, it's better than nothing. These savings might be needed for car repairs, unexpected travel, holidays, presents or replacing essentials in your home.

'No matter how tight your budget is, try to save something. Even if you can only manage £10 or £20 a month, it's better than nothing.'

There are lots of saving schemes offered by banks and building societies – some give much better interest rates than others, depending on whether you can save a set amount each month, or can commit to leaving your money there for a set period. Shop around and see what suits you best. If you arrange a standing order into a savings account, the money will gradually accumulate, without you having to worry about remembering to transfer the money.

Don't forget ISAs which offer tax-free interest. A cash ISA savings account allows you to save up to £3,600 per year, tax free. Everyone is entitled to one cash ISA account. However, be aware that if you deposit £3,600 into your account in any one year, and then withdraw, for example £100, you can't then replace that £100 until the beginning of the next tax year. This is because your account has logged that at some point of the year it reached the £3,600 limit. Also, if you do not use your £3,600 allowance, you cannot carry it over the next tax year.

Summing Up

▪ Make sure you know your annual and monthly net incomes.

▪ Be realistic about your outgoings – do not underestimate.

▪ Set up bank accounts, direct debits and standing orders where applicable.

▪ Keep a record of everything you spend for a few months so you can see where your money goes and any areas where you might be able to save.

▪ Resist the temptation of credit cards unless you pay them off in full each month.

▪ If you plan on sharing a house, establish a system for paying bills and household essentials early on.

Chapter Two

Rent or Buy, and Where?

When you first live independently, you will have the choice of buying or renting a property. Your decision will depend very much on your finances, as buying tends to be more expensive and a mortgage can be difficult to get, though this will vary according to which part of the country you live in. In order to obtain a mortgage, you will need to prove you are credit worthy, that your income can cover the repayments, and that you are able to provide the deposit required by your mortgage lender.

Let's think about the financial implications of these.

Buying

Buying a property is a major decision and you need to take many factors into account to avoid it becoming an expensive mistake. When you buy, you commit to a monthly mortgage plus other essential outgoings. Mortgage interest rates can rise or fall, so you will never be certain how much your mortgage will be, unless you take a fixed rate mortgage; this is when the interest rate is fixed for a determined period of a year or more.

The costs of buying

It is more expensive to buy a property than rent as you will have to pay for surveys, solicitor's fees and, depending on the cost of your home, possibly stamp duty. If you decide to sell your home, you will have to pay for an estate agent and a Home Information Pack (HIP) survey. You may not be able to sell for many months, so you won't be able to release your income to buy elsewhere.

The benefits of buying

- Buying allows you to invest your money into a property which may appreciate in value.

- As an owner, you have more freedom to make changes to your home, including alterations and decor.

- You may feel more secure as you do not have a lease which has to be renewed every few months.

Shared buying

'Many young people buy a property with a friend. It is a cheaper financial option and you have the benefits of owning – but at the cost of renting.'

Local housing schemes enable you to buy and rent at the same time. This usually means that you only own part of the property, with the option of buying more in time. This is a cheaper than buying outright, with a smaller deposit, but you need to look carefully at the agreement to determine how much you will own after a certain period of time, and what happens if you want to move.

Buying with a friend

Many young people buy a property with a friend. It is a cheaper financial option and you have the benefits of owning – but at the cost of renting. However, you need a legal agreement which covers you both should one of you want to move, so that the property is either sold or you have the option to buy the other share.

This arrangement can work, but it can be tricky unless you get the legal framework right. You also need to be very careful about your relationship, as a beautiful friendship can easily deteriorate when you are both living in close proximity.

For more detailed information on buying a property, please see chapter 10.

The advantages and disadvantages of sharing a home

Advantages

- It is often the cheapest option.
- In most instances, everyone shares the utility bills and other fixed outgoings, such as the rent, equally.
- If you are setting out on your own for the first time, sharing can offer you company and an easy way to make friends.
- If you are outgoing and enjoy company, are easygoing and adaptable, then house sharing might suit you very nicely.

Disadvantages

- You might want your own space and privacy and not want to share a lounge, kitchen and bathroom.
- If the others want to party every night and you are a quiet person, it won't work. If they work shifts, come in late and you have an early start, it could be tricky.

To help you make a decision on whether house sharing is for you, you should ask yourself what kind of characters would you like to share with and what kind of privacy arrangements you'd prefer. It is a good idea to take your time viewing house shares until you find the right people to share with.

House or flat?

If you are buying a property, you might have very definite views on what you want, but consider the following:

Houses

- A house will need more upkeep – and this costs money.

- You will need to consider maintaining the outside of the property, as well as the inside.

- Houses tend to have gardens and you will need to maintain these. Great if you like gardening or an outside space.

- You are likely to have more space, possibly a driveway for cars and a garage, though some purpose built flats have these too.

- You are less likely to hear noise from adjoining properties, though if you have a terraced house you will have neighbours on each side.

Flats

- Flats do not involve so much upkeep, though you may have to contribute to a residents' maintenance scheme for annual repairs to the building.

- Flats can be more secure as they have one entrance and many have entry phone systems or access codes on the doors. If you are likely to spend time travelling or be away from home for extended periods, flats can offer a more secure option.

- You are unlikely to have a garden unless you have a ground floor flat, but some flats can have verandas or roof gardens.

- Your utility bills will tend to be lower, as most modern purpose built flats require less heating than a house and council tax will almost always be lower.

- Noise could be a factor as you are likely to have neighbours above, below and on each side, unless you have a flat on the corner of a block or on the top floor.

Renting

Renting a property can be a cheaper and more flexible option if you are not sure how long you want to be in an area or if your circumstances are likely to change unexpectedly. You will not need such a large deposit, your monthly rent is set for a period of at least six months in most cases, making budgeting easier, and you will not be responsible for the upkeep or the fabric of the building.

You can rent on your own, with a friend or with a group of people – you'll be able to choose from a house with several bedrooms or a smaller flat, whatever suits your circumstances.

One of your main decisions will be whether to rent an unfurnished or furnished property. There are advantages and disadvantages to both. If the property is furnished, you will not have the outlay associated with buying beds, sofas, furnishings and possibly white goods. However, neither will you have any choice over the furniture in the property.

You will find a huge difference in furnished accommodation; some will be newly furnished and with modern furniture, while other properties will have older and more traditional furniture, possibly showing signs of wear and tear. Take your time choosing, and take into consideration the cost of furnishing the property if you were to buy everything you needed.

Some landlords provide white goods – a washing machine, cooker and fridge – but no furniture or curtains. These properties are usually classed as unfurnished with white goods, and can be a good compromise.

What to look for when choosing your home

The following points are relevant whether you are renting or buying. Remember that if you buy, you will most probably be living with these 'factors' for longer, so think carefully.

Location

- Is the area safe to live in?

- Would you feel safe coming and going at night on your own?

- What do you know about the area?

- Have you driven or walked around at night?

- Is there good street lighting and safe parking?

- Are there any properties or businesses near that could be noisy, such as pubs, clubs, restaurants or lots of student houses?

- Is it near a busy road?

- Are there any alleyways or other types of paths very close to the property?

- Is there access from the front and rear and is it safe?

- Is it near a doctor's surgery or health centre?

- Can you walk to the supermarket or do you need a car or other transport?

Essentials to consider

- Water – is your water supply on a meter or is it a fixed charge?

- Council tax – which band does the property fall into and how much is this each month?

- Central heating – gas central heating or electric heating? Is the property connected to gas and electric or is it just electric? You want to know this before you start purchasing appliances like your cooker!

- Parking – do you have a garage or driveway and if not, can you park safely and legally on the street?

- Neighbours – you can't choose your neighbours, but you can avoid properties where the neighbours are noisy; if they operate a noisy business of any kind or if they have noisy animals, for example. It is worth asking the person you are buying or renting from who lives next door. They might not elaborate if there are problems, but try to find out as much as you can.

- Landlords – is the landlord friendly and efficient? Can the current tenants tell you? Does the landlord carry out repairs quickly, and do they ensure the property is well looked after?

- Survey – have you had a structural survey done if you are buying the property? Which level of survey have you chosen? Do you need to offset any work against the purchase price?

- Kitchens and bathrooms – what condition are they in? Would they need replacing?

- Carpets – are the carpets included in the house if you are buying? Would you need to replace them or are they in reasonable condition?

- What is the property's energy rating? Ask for a copy of your home's HIP – either from the estate agent, if you're buying, or your landlord.

How do you find your flat or house?

If you are going to university or are already at university, there should be a student accommodation office where you can get help and advice on anything accommodation-related. You can usually advertise for flat-sharers or look for houses from landlords as well. These adverts are often placed in the accommodation office, but many universities put the details on their websites where current students can access the information.

Other places to look for accommodation both for renting and buying include:

- Local estate agents and websites such as www.rightmove.co.uk.

- Local newspapers.

- Adverts in shop windows.

- Word of mouth.

'If you are going to university or are already at university, there should be a student accommodation office where you can get help and advice on anything accommodation-related.'

Legal stuff if you rent

You will be given tenancy agreement to sign by your landlord. This will include their policies on some of the following:

- What you can and cannot use the property for.

- Whether you can keep pets.

- Whether you are allowed to sub-let.

- An inventory of items in the property and what condition they're in.

- Any responsibility you have to maintain the garden or the fabric of the building.

- What could be deducted from your deposit when you leave, for cleaning or repairs.

- How long you can live there and how much notice both you and the landlord needs to give.

- A review date for rent increases or any changes.

'If you are not sure of anything in the lease take it to the Citizens Advice Bureau, or your university accommodation office, for advice.'

It is important that you fully understand your tenancy agreement as it protects both you and the landlord. If you are not sure of anything in the lease, take it to the Citizens Advice Bureau, or your university accommodation office, for advice.

Summing Up

- Think carefully about the advantages and disadvantages of flats and houses.

- Choose the area carefully.

- Obtain receipts for any money that exchanges hands.

- If possible, find out if the landlord is reputable from previous tenants.

- Check your tenancy agreement carefully.

- Check your house inventory thoroughly.

- Consult your student accommodation office if you need any advice or need anyone to check your tenancy agreement.

- If you are unsure of anything, consult the Citizens Advice Bureau for free help.

Chapter Three

Buying Furniture and Appliances

Buying furniture for your first home is exciting – you can indulge your own tastes without having to live with what other people have chosen for you! Even if you are sharing a house or flat, you can add personal touches to your room at least. So, how can you make your money stretch as far as possible? Try to buy second-hand when shopping for furniture and appliances; there are a lot of great deals around. If you can't get what you want second-hand, there are also some good value chain stores you can try.

- Ebay – www.ebay.co.uk.
- Freecycle – www.uk.freecycle.org.
- Local free papers.
- Notices in shop windows.
- Charity shops.
- Auction rooms.
- Friends – ask them to donate anything unwanted.
- Stores such as Ikea and Argos.
- Sales – best in January and July.

'Try to buy second-hand when shopping for furniture and appliances; there are a lot of great deals around. If you can't get what you want second-hand, there are also some good value chain stores you can try.'

The essentials – what to buy for an unfurnished home

Bedroom

- Bed frame and mattress plus duvet, pillows and bed linen.
- Wardrobe and chest of drawers, although sometimes these are already built in to the bedroom.
- Bedside table.
- Mirror.

Living room

- Sofa or sofa bed, chairs.
- TV and CD/radio equipment.

Kitchen

- Cooker (in rented accommodation this may be provided).
- Fridge freezer.
- Washing machine.
- Kitchen utensils.
- Towels.
- Ironing board and iron.
- Vacuum cleaner.

Bathroom

- Towels.

- Laundry basket.
- Mirror.
- Bathroom cabinet, shelving or storage containers.

All rooms

- Curtains, blinds, carpets and rugs, if needed.

How to choose what will suit your lifestyle

Think about who will be using your home and how it will be used:

- Will you have lots of visitors?
- Will people occasionally stay overnight?
- Do you have any pets?
- What is the layout of your home like?

What should you buy second-hand?

You can save a huge amount of money buying second-hand, but there are times when it is not a good idea. So what's a good second-hand bargain and what isn't?

The only item where you really should try to buy new is your bed, mainly for hygiene reasons. If you like a wooden bedstead, then by all means buy it second-hand, but buy a new mattress. Matresses can be quite expensive, but it is worth investing in a good one that will last longer than a basic cheap one. White goods such as cookers, fridges, washing machines and vacuum cleaners can be good second-hand buys. Sometimes people are emigrating or simply moving to a home with built-in appliances, and the white goods they are selling are almost new. Try looking on Ebay or Freecycle for these.

Remember, you are unlikely to get any guarantees with second-hand goods, so make sure they work before you part with your cash.

'Remember, you are unlikely to get any guarantees with second-hand goods, so make sure they work before you part with your cash.'

If you'll have lots of visitors, think about the colour of carpets and furnishings. Pale colours look great, but will they be practical for your home? If you plan to party a lot or have lots of visitors, pale cream carpets may soon become a nightmare. If it is possible, consider wood or laminate floors with rugs. You will have to pay for the laying of them, unless you are good at DIY of course, but they could be more economical than replacing carpets in the longer term. If you are renting, it may not be possible to change integral features such as carpets, so you should check with your landlord before planning any major jobs.

If you are buying a sofa, ask yourself if a sofa bed is a better idea. That way you can always offer friends a bed. If so, don't go for the cheapest, which are often made with a foam mattress; very quickly these will sag and your guests will not have a good night's rest. This is one item not worth economising on. Choose washable covers if possible, so you can easily freshen it up.

Remember – if you are renting, find out what comes with your house/flat before you get too carried away with buying!

Moving in

Packing in advance

When you know the moving-in date, you need to arrange some kind of transport. Depending on your accommodation, this might be a car load or a lorry load! You have three options:

- Your own transport, with friends' help.
- Hire a van.
- Use a removal company.

If you need a hire van or removal company, obtain at least three quotes. You might be surprised at the variation! Recommendation is always a good idea. Remember that the removal company can pack for you too, though this will increase the cost.

If you plan on moving everything yourself, start collecting suitable containers such as boxes and old newspapers to use for packing. When you pack, it's a good idea to label the boxes and containers, and to try to keep as many items for each room together. You'll be thankful for your oganisation in the end!

You might want to keep any delicate or valuable items in your possession and take them in your own car if you have one.

The person who is moving out of the property should thoroughly clean it before you are due to move in; however, depending on the condition, you may want to give it a once over yourself. If you have a larger budget, or the property really requires it, you could hire a cleaning company.

If needed, it might be worth considering taking measurements in advance for curtains and blinds, so that you can buy or order them before you move in; they can take a while to be made to measure if you have large or odd-shaped windows. If you want to buy ready made then you might have to cut them to fit, so do as much as you can beforehand – but not until you are absolutely certain the home is yours!

On the day

Make up a box of essentials including a kettle, tea, coffee, milk, sugar, cups/mugs, biscuits and some cutlery. Take these in your car, rather than including them in your removal van, or worse, hidden away under everything else you have packed. Once you start unpacking, you will be ready for some refreshments, and so will the removal team or your friends!

Summing Up

- If you have a limited budget, search around for second-hand furniture/appliances.

- Start collecting boxes or containers for your move early.

- Take measurements before you buy anything to ensure it will fit.

- Arrange transport for moving as soon as possible.

- Make a refreshments box so that you can have a drink and a snack as soon as you arrive.

Chapter Four

Decorating and Making Your House a Home

If you are renting a flat or house, check your lease or the letting agent to find out if you are allowed to decorate. Some landlords are very happy for you to decorate; others will stipulate it has to be tasteful; others will insist you put it all back to the original colours when you leave. Whatever you do, don't go ahead unless you have checked, otherwise you could be in breach of the terms of your lease.

If you want to decorate your room in a shared house, or at university, then the same applies – check that it's allowed.

If you're buying your own home, then the choice is all yours!

Decorating your room to your taste can make it feel more like home, but before you pick up that paintbrush, there are a few points worth considering.

'Light colours give the illusion of more space and dark colours make rooms look smaller.'

Decorating tips

Adding your own choice of colour to your home is exciting and makes it feel more like yours – whether you are renting or buying. Your choice of colours is personal, but it's worth keeping in mind some tips.

Light colours give the illusion of more space and dark colours make rooms look smaller. Most modern homes are short of space, so making the rooms look larger is the trick. Also, if your home is open plan, it makes sense to keep the same wall colour throughout to avoid a patchwork effect.

Before you splash out on paint, buy some testers. Colours look very different on walls compared with shade cards, and they often come out darker on the wall, so you might want to go lighter than you think you need. Remember to use the tester in the room you intend to paint, as light makes a huge difference to depth of colour.

Different rooms and different surfaces need different paint.

- Kitchens and bathrooms need a paint which you can wipe clean and that will withstand moisture; in other words, you need a paint that's not matte. This is usually called eggshell, although there are other names for this type of paint. Eggshell has a very slight sheen to it.

- Other areas of the house can take matte emulsion or you can use a wipe-clean paint if you want.

- Woodwork, such as skirting boards, cupboards and doors, is usually painted with gloss paint. This is so you can easily wipe clean, but you can use emulsion or semi-gloss if you prefer the finish.

Gloss paint is slightly trickier to apply than matte – you tend to see the brush strokes if you aren't careful – and it can run, so practise on something that isn't seen very much to begin with. You can paint the woodwork the same colour as the walls, a shade or two lighter or darker, or a completely different colour. Try to avoid a really stark contrast as it tends to make the room look smaller.

Preparation before you begin to paint is very important. So, before you even open that tin of paint:

- Rub down old paint surfaces with sand paper where the paint is flaking or uneven.

- Fill any cracks or holes in the walls with a filler solution and rub down until smooth.

- Use bleach or mould-remover to clean any areas that show signs of damp or condensation, such as in the bathroom.

- Wash paintwork and dust walls, to remove dirt and grease.

- Make sure all surfaces are clean and dry before you paint them.

It is boring, hard work and may seem pointless – but you do need to do this to get a good result. You will need sandpaper in rough and smooth grades, ready-mixed or powder filler, detergent, mould-remover or bleach, dusters and cleaning cloths and some rubber gloves to protect your hands. All of this can be bought at your local DIY store.

Don't forget obvious things like moving as much furniture out of the room as possible, or covering up anything that can't be moved with dustsheets. You can buy dustsheets or large plastic sheeting, but it is cheaper to use something you might already have, or can scrounge from friends and family – old sheeting, bedspreads – anything that is big enough to drape over furniture. If you are painting with a roller, be aware that small splatters of paint can spread a long way, so cover everything up well if you don't want it paint-splashed!

If you find it hard to keep a steady hard while painting, use masking tape around light switches and plugs to ensure it looks neat and tidy when finished. You might need to apply several coats of paint to cover a dark or brightly painted wall – most walls will need two coats anyway to prevent it looking patchy.

If you are painting a bedroom, remember that the smell of paint lingers. Open the windows, paint early in the day if you are going to sleep in the room, or sleep in another room until the decorating is completed.

Accessories

Adding a few personal touches to your room or house will make a huge difference. You do not need to spend a fortune for everything to look more homely. Unless you are starting completely from scratch, you will have some items from home to add to your new room or home. Think of ornaments, books, posters, photographs and plants.

Decide what you want and, if you are short of cash, think about where you can buy these items cheaply. Charity and junk shops are an option, as well as larger chain stores that sell household items.

Some items that give a personal touch include:

'Decide what you want and, if you are short of cash, think about where you can buy these items cheaply. Charity and junk shops are an option as well as larger chain stores that sell household items.'

- Pictures.
- Rugs.
- Candles.
- Vases.
- Framed photographs.
- Books.
- Plants.
- Lighting.
- Shelves.

Pictures

If you have a small room, you will find that one or two large pictures or posters create more impact than several small ones. Alternatively, you could group together several smaller pictures. Avoid dotting lots of small pictures around the walls as they won't really make much impact.

Take care not to damage the walls. If you are renting a home, your landlord might not want lots of holes in the walls from picture hooks or allow the use of Blu Tac which can leave marks on walls – so check your lease first. If in doubt, contact them to double-check or ask permission, particularly for hanging pictures.

Rugs

Rugs can bring some colour into otherwise neutral rooms. They are also useful for covering worn patches of carpets and stains, as well as protecting carpets where a lot of wear is likely. Tone them in with existing colours, or introduce some bright colours if you want some contrast. The most expensive is pure wool, but you can buy man-made and cotton rugs quite cheaply from stores such as Ikea (which is worth a walk round for inspiration!).

- A word of warning – if you put brightly coloured rugs onto a light-coloured carpet, ensure that the colour from the rug doesn't transfer. You can use a paper liner underneath to prevent this, which is well worth remembering before your landlord chases you for a new carpet!

Safety – rugs look cosy, but they can be dangerous. If they are in hallways, make sure they won't slip or that people could trip over the edges, especially if the edges curl up after a time. For the same reasons, don't have rugs on stair landings or kitchens as anyone slipping and falling could have a nasty accident.

Candles

Candles can make attractive ornaments, whether lit or not. As with pictures, several large candles grouped together can look stunning.

- If you do light the candles, place them on a safe surface, where they can't fall over or set light to anything flammable such as curtains, clothes, books or paper. Do check they are extinguished when you leave the room for any longer than a few minutes.

Lighting

Lighting is essential for a cosy room and creating atmosphere. If your room or home needs a lick of paint, then some well-chosen lamps will soften the appearance until you can decorate. As well as your overhead light, you will need either table lamps, desk lamps or larger floor lamps. Softer lighting can transform even the dullest room. You might need to experiment with what suits the rooms best.

When buying lamps, always check the maximum bulb wattage they take. It is no good buying a lamp that takes only 60 watts if you need a bright light. Halogen bulbs give a very bright light which is useful for desk-work.

- From a style perspective, larger table lamps look better in a living room than smaller lamps, space permitting.

- Uplighters are very effective and take up little space if your room is small.

Plants

Even if you don't have a garden, or much of one, you can make your home attractive with plants. The smallest room can be brightened with a flowering plant – and if the plant or greenery is edible, so much the better.

Plants can transform a room. Again, a large plant which is a feature of the room can be very striking. Think about positioning plants to hide anything in the room which you don't want to see. You can also use large plants to divide a room, by creating a living screen. Take into account the conditions that plants need; some need lots of light, others prefer shade – and the same applies to watering them!

■ Don't forget that plants grow! What starts off as a small specimen could eventually reach six feet high or more. Have you got enough space for it? Choosing the wrong plant or the wrong place can be an expensive mistake. The BBC gardening website has some useful information – see www.bbc. co.uk/gardening. Use the search facility on their homepage for information on looking after houseplants.

What to grow

As well as the many household plants that are available, you can also consider:

■ Potting up a few bulbs into containers in the autumn for spring colour, or buying ready-made containers of bulbs from the supermarket.

■ Growing some herbs in pots on your windowsills. Picking your own herbs is very satisfying when you're on a budget!

Shelves

If you run out of floor space for your possessions, think vertical. It is possible to buy shelves in all sizes, designs and materials: wood, acrylic, glass, metal. Shelves can make a real difference to your room. They add extra space and a focal point for anything you want to display – books, photos, ornaments.

When fixing shelves in place, you must ensure that there are no electrical wires or water pipes behind the walls where the screws will go. You can buy a detector to test for this, which bleeps when it traces something behind the wall. Do not drill into your walls too close to electrical sockets before you have established what is in the wall. If you're renting, you should check with your landlord to ensure you're allowed to make any modifications – particularly if they require making holes in the walls!

Summing Up

■ Check with your landlord whether you can decorate your room, flat or house.

■ Good preparation is the key to a good finish when painting.

■ Buy the correct type of paint for the room.

■ Choose colours carefully to maximise space and light in your home.

■ Personal touches need not be expensive.

■ Look in markets and cheap chain stores for some bargains.

Chapter Five

Safety, Security and Emergencies

Safety

When you move into your own home, whether that is a single room, a house or a flat, there are safety issues you must consider.

Fire

Your home should be fitted with a smoke alarm. If you're living in a house or flat, you will need one on the landing and another in the downstairs hall. If you're moving into student halls, your room should come with one as standard – make sure you check this. Smoke alarms are cheap and easy to install, but they only work if they have a battery that works, so check it regularly. Check the battery once a month – such as on the 1st of each month – and change the battery twice a year.

A fire extinguisher and a fire blanket can be very useful in the kitchen. If your home is rented, these may be provided, but if not they are worth considering.

You should reduce the risk of fires by taking simple precautions:

- Appliances – do not go to bed leaving on any electrical appliances such as washing machines, tumble driers, cookers and certain electric heaters.
- Check plugs and cables on appliances and if there is any sign of fraying or damage, have them repaired or replaced.

'Smoke alarms are cheap and easy to install, but they only work if they have a battery that works, so check it regularly.'

- Do not overload electrical sockets by having too many appliances plugged into one socket.

- Do not use tea light candles unless they are in a suitable holder.

- Ensure that any heaters you use are well away from furnishings, and that nothing can fall onto them and cover them.

- Do not leave pans, especially chip pans or frying pans, on the cooker if you are not in the room.

- Make sure that tea towels, towels and oven gloves are not too near the cooker, or that they can be blown onto the burners.

- Ensure that curtains or other furnishings cannot blow onto cookers, candles or other naked flames.

- If you have an open fire, always use a spark guard if you are not in the room, and ensure it is carefully in place if you go out or to bed and the fire is still burning.

- If anyone in your home smokes, ensure that all ash trays are emptied safely each night and cigarettes extinguished.

- Furniture should be fire-retardant. Legally, your landlord should only furnish your house with fire-retardant furniture and should show you a fire certificate. It is important to check this.

- Close all internal doors at night so that if a fire starts it is contained in one room for as long as possible.

- If you suspect a fire by smelling smoke, or the door feels hot, do not open the door to the room. Call the emergency services and get anyone else out of the property.

- More people are killed by smoke than flames. If you smell smoke and cannot escape, the safest place is on the floor. Try to cover any gaps under doors to avoid smoke entering the room. Open or break windows if you have to.

- Escape routes – if you're living in a shared house, and especially if you are on a top floor of a building, work out an escape route if there is a fire. You need to consider that there may be no lights, so you should know where the exits are, and the quickest and safest route outside. As a group you could discuss this. Be aware of double glazed windows as exits – some do not have enough space for you to escape, and it is unlikely the glass could be broken.

Carbon monoxide

Poisoning from carbon monoxide is a hazard if you have faulty gas central heating or an old gas boiler. Tragically, some young people – mainly students living in rented accommodation – have died from this poisoning. The gas has no smell, but it makes people feel sick and unwell, with symptoms similar to colds, flu and food poisoning, and it can be fatal if you inhale it whilst sleeping.

If you're renting, your landlord should have a certificate to show that the building has passed a test showing it is safe. If not, don't rent the property unless an up-to-date certificate is provided.

You can buy testers for carbon monoxide very cheaply, which you can put in your home as another precaution.

If you suspect carbon monoxide poisoning, get everyone out of the building and open the windows. Call 999 if anyone is unconscious and go to Accident and Emergency if you feel unwell.

Water

Do you know where the stopcock is? This is where the mains water comes into the house. If there is ever any flooding from a burst pipe, or you cannot turn off the water at the tap, then you will need to turn off the stopcock. They are often located under the stairs, in a cupboard, or somewhere that is not immediately visible. So don't wait until there is an emergency before you find it. If you're buying, this is a question you can ask the previous owners or your estate agent; if you're renting, make sure you ask your landlord.

'You can buy testers for carbon monoxide very cheaply, which you can put in your home as another precaution.'

Electrics

There will be a fuse box in your house. If there is a problem with an electrical appliance, then a fuse might blow. In order to repair it, you will have to know where your fuse box is, and have some spare fuses. Again, check this out before an emergency occurs. If any major faults occur with anything electrical, call out a qualified electrician or, in the case of old and cheap appliances such as kettles, irons and toasters, it is better to get rid of them and buy new.

- For advice on how to change a plug, fuses and other DIY tips, see www.ultimatehandyman.co.uk. If you are in any doubt, always ask for advice from a professional or someone who knows what they're doing!

Security

Keeping your possessions and home safe and secure is vital. Many insurance companies will not cover your possessions unless certain security steps are in place.

- Locks – you should have good locks to the doors and windows of your room or house. A deadlock on the main front and back door is best as well as the usual Yale lock. If you're sharing a property then think about having a lock on your room door. In a shared property, many insurance companies will not insure your belongings unless your room has a lock. Window locks are essential if you live on the ground floor of a building. But locks are no good unless they are used – so don't forget to use them each time you go out!

- Door chain – a door chain can be very useful either on a single room or on a front door, so you can see who is there before you open the door.

- Lights – leave a light on if you are going out for the evening and want to give the impression there is someone at home. You can buy timers which will turn the light on and off at a pre-set time if you're away for a significant amount of time.

- If your home or room has a solid door, have a peephole installed so you can see who is outside before you open the door.

- Keep valuables out of sight from passers-by. This means your lap top, hi-fi equipment, money, jewellery, mobile phone, etc.

- Think about buying a safe box. This is a metal, fireproof filing box in which you can keep important documents like your passport, birth certificate, insurance details and bank statements.

- Keys – never leave a spare key in an obvious place such as under a plant pot at the front door – burglars know where to look! If you are worried that you might be locked out, why not leave a spare key with a trusted neighbour or friend?

Outside your home there may also be steps you can take to make it safer. Unless your lease or landlord prohibits this, cut back any overhanging trees or shrubs which obscure the view of doors from the footpath outside. These could provide cover for a burglar. They also make it safer for you as you enter your home late at night. You could consider fitting outside security lights that come on when anyone passes, and you should ensure that any gates that are not used regularly are bolted or locked.

Personal safety – getting to and from your home

If you are renting or buying for the first time, you might not have too much choice over where you live if your choice is determined by cost. Some parts of towns and cities are safer than others. Until you know your surroundings well (and even when you do), you should take as many precautions as possible to stay safe. Most of these include precautions you will have used for many years already, but it is always worth reminding yourself. These include:

- Avoid walking home alone late at night, especially if you do not know the area well.

- Always take the main route where there are other people. Don't take short cuts across parks, waste ground, unlit footpaths and anywhere you cannot be seen or call for help.

- Carry a personal alarm.

- Avoid taking lifts in unlicensed taxis, or from anyone saying they are a taxi service.

- Be aware when using public transport – sit near the driver or other people.

- Tell friends what time you expect to be home at night.

- Don't invite strangers into your home, no matter how kind or helpful they appear to be.

- Don't disclose your personal details (such as your address) to complete strangers.

- If you do have to travel home alone, be sober enough to defend yourself in a dangerous situation.

- Avoid arguments and situations with strangers that are confrontational, whether you are alone or with a group of friends.

- If you travel by bike or car, ensure you have the basics on hand to carry out repairs, or be able to call someone to help you if you are stranded.

- Think about doing a basic self-defence course – they are often run for women only.

'Avoid taking lifts in unlicensed taxis, or from anyone saying they are a taxi service.'

Insurance

Most insurance companies will cover your possessions whether you are a student, sharing a property or living in your own house or flat. If you are a student, you may be covered already on your parents' home contents insurance. Usually your term-time accommodation must be classed as temporary and you need to fulfil certain conditions such as having a lock on your room. Read the small print though to find out the maximum cover on items, and whether there are any exclusions.

If you are insuring your entire home, then you need to know the total value of your house contents. Be careful not to underestimate – your premium will be lower but you may not be covered for the replacement of items if you need to make a claim. If anyone else will be sharing your home and paying you rent then you need to discuss the implications with your insurers.

Dealing with emergencies

If any emergencies occur, it is essential that you know how to deal with them quickly.

- Make a list of all the telephone numbers you might need in an emergency and put them into your phone and have a list pinned up in your accommodation as well.

- Some suggestions would be emergency services, GP surgery and out of hours number, next of kin, landlord, numbers in case of lost/stolen bank cards, gas, water and electric suppliers, plumber, electrician and locksmith.

Security

If you lock yourself out of your room or home, or lose your keys, these are your options:

- Contact your friends if they have a key.

- If you're renting, contact your landlord or student accommodation office.

- Contact a locksmith to open the doors for you.

- If there is a fire hazard or an electrical appliance left on in your room or in the building, contact the emergency services.

Money

If you lose your bank or credit cards or have them stolen, you should report this to your bank without delay. If they have been stolen, you should also contact the police. The bank will have a helpline number for this. If you have any money or possessions stolen, you should contact the police and your insurers.

Appliances

If your washing machine or any other appliances break down, what action you take depends on whether you own the appliance or the landlord does.

If you own the appliance, check whether it is under the manufacturer's guarantee, which normally lasts for between one to three years. If it is, contact either the supplier or the manufacturer. There should be instructions on the guarantee telling you what to do.

If you do not own the appliance, contact your landlord. You might already know what the procedure is, but if not, make sure. They should either arrange for someone to come and repair or replace it, or ask you to do so and they will cover the costs. Under no circumstances should you arrange for repairs until you have spoken to your landlord, as you could be asked to foot the bill.

Quotations – if you want an appliance repaired, arrange for at least three quotations as they can vary enormously. Ensure that the person is qualified and able to carry out the work. Do not pay anything in advance, and avoid calling them out as an emergency unless absolutely necessary as the costs will be higher.

> 'If you smell gas, or suspect a gas leak, get everyone out of the property. Do not switch on the lights, smoke, or do anything that might make a spark as it could cause an explosion.'

Gas, water and electric

Contact details for these utility companies are in the phone book and on your bills.

If you smell gas, or suspect a gas leak, get everyone out of the property. Do not switch on the lights, smoke or do anything that might make a spark as it could cause an explosion.

If there is a burst pipe, turn off the water at the stopcock – locate this before you need to. If there is a flood, move anything electrical away and use old towels to mop up the water.

If you lose your electric supply, phone your utility provider to report it. If there is a problem with an appliance, do not try to fix it yourself; turn the electricity off at the fuse box and call an electrician.

Summing Up

- Take care of your personal safety, especially in new areas.

- Ensure your home is secure with proper locks and use them.

- Insure your possessions.

- Ask to see fire certificates and carbon monoxide certificates.

- Test the batteries of smoke detectors regularly.

- Buy a carbon monoxide tester.

- Have emergency telephone numbers stored.

- Switch off appliances when you go out and don't run them overnight.

- If you are renting and any appliances break down, check your lease first before you repair anything.

Chapter Six

Looking After Your Home

Once you are settled in your own home, you will want to keep it looking good. Even if you don't relish cleaning, you will have to do some. You will find that if you tackle the dirt little and often, it is much easier than having a huge clean up every now and then.

Food poisoning

If you don't keep your kitchen and bathroom clean, you could be at risk from food poisoning. Food poisoning occurs from one of two main sources:

- Uncooked or cooked foods which harbour harmful bacteria and toxins.
- Bacteria and viruses transferred from people's hands onto food, cutlery and work surfaces.

Raw meat and undercooked chicken can cause food poisoning. Always ensure that chicken is cooked through and no traces of pink, uncooked meat remain. If you ever reheat it, ensure it is piping hot.

Cooked rice which is left in a warm place for several hours can develop dangerous levels of bacteria. These bacteria develop from spores in the uncooked rice which are not killed during cooking. When the rice is cooked and left at room temperature, the bacteria multiply. All cooked rice should be refrigerated within an hour of cooking, and reheated until steaming hot if you want to eat it hot again. Do not keep cooked rice in the fridge for more than one day.

Cross-contamination is another cause of food poisoning. This means that if you chop raw meat such as chicken on a chopping board, then use the board again for bread or vegetables without washing it in hot soapy water, you risk bacteria from the meat being transferred onto other food that may be eaten raw. Ideally, have two boards – one for meat and another for everything else.

Bacteria from people's hands can also cause food poisoning. The most common bacteria is e.coli, which is found in our bowels. This is why it is important to practice good personal hygiene, and also to wash all raw fruit and vegetables before eating as they may have bacteria on from other people's hands.

Keeping work surfaces clean is another factor in avoiding upset stomachs. If you have touched cupboard handles or utensils after touching raw meat, the surfaces should be washed with diluted bleach.

There are so many products that can make cleaning quick and easy, but you don't need to spend a lot to get good results. There is no need to spend a fortune on different cleaning products; many multipurpose products can be used in most rooms. So, what do you need to clean, how often and with what?

Sharing the chores

If you are sharing your home, then it is a good idea to think about having a system so that you – or a housemate – does not do all the housework. If you do not organise this early on, it can breed resentment!

If you will be doing all the cleaning yourselves, draw up a list of chores and divide them equally – for example, one person will dust and vacuum the lounge once a week, while another will do the hall, stairs and landing. It should go without saying that everyone cleans the bathroom after use, and also leaves the kitchen clean and tidy – nothing can annoy other people more than finding every pan and utensil dirty in the sink when they want to cook! Be considerate to others.

Cleaning jobs for every room

- Vacuuming or floor washing.
- Dusting.
- Window cleaning.
- Wiping paint work or work surfaces.
- Dusting or wiping curtains and blinds.

Bedroom

- Vacuum once a week or more if necessary. Make sure you vacuum under the bed where a lot of dust collects.

- Mop floors that are not carpeted once a week.

- Dust once a week. Use a duster that is slightly damp to pick up dust, and always dust from the highest point first and work down.

- Wash your bed sheets and duvet cover once a week.

- If your duvet gets grubby or spills occur, check the label to see if it's machine washable or take it to the dry cleaners.

- If you spill drinks on your duvet, put an elastic band around the wet area, then gently wash that part only by hand and dry it.

- Clean the inside of your windows regularly, perhaps every couple of months.

- Once or twice a year, take everything out of your wardrobe, dust the shelves and vacuum inside.

Living room

How often you vacuum will depend on how many people are in your house. You might need to do it once or twice a week. Some of the following needs to be done regularly, others just once every few months.

- Vacuum all crumbs, dust and dirt as soon as possible, otherwise they will be trodden into the carpets. Leave any wet mud to dry first.

- Dust surfaces.

- Spillages – if you spill drinks on your carpet, act fast. Blot up as much as possible with paper towels, or a clean tea towel. Use a suitable carpet cleaning product to spot-clean the area or, if you don't have any, use water.

- Take the seat and back cushions off your sofa occasionally and vacuum the base with the attachments that fit your vacuum cleaner. You will be surprised how much dust, crumbs and various items are under there.

'You will find that if you tackle the dirt little and often it is much easier than having a huge clean up every now and then.'

- Once or twice a year, move large furniture, such as sofas and wardrobes, so you can vacuum and dust behind them.

- Dust your skirting boards and vacuum right along the edges of the carpet.

- Dust lampshades.

- If you have pictures or mirrors in the room, dust the frames and clean the glass.

What to use

- Vacuum cleaner.

- Dusters.

- Mop.

Optional

- Spray polish.

- Cleaners for windows and mirrors.

- Carpet cleaner for spills.

Bathroom

If you share a bathroom, then it should always be cleaned regularly after each use. If you can, keep the cleaning products in the bathroom so they are on hand.

- Air the room by opening the window every day to keep mould and damp at a minimum.

- Clean the bath, basin or shower every time you use it, especially if you share your home with others. A quick spray with a bathroom cleaner will prevent a build-up of limescale and dirt.

- Clean tiles around the bath or shower regularly to prevent build-up of limescale and mould.

- Clean the toilet properly at least once a week. A splash of bleach now and then is not enough. Lift the seat and lid and clean with diluted bleach or

54

an antibacterial spray cleaner. Clean the seat and lid the same way. Don't forget the flush which can carry bacteria. Put neat bleach down into the toilet bowl regularly and try to leave it overnight.

- Clean the floor around the toilet regularly, either washing the floor or washing pedestal mats.
- Mop the bathroom floor weekly or vacuum if carpeted.
- Change bathmats, pedestal mats and towels weekly.
- If you have a shower curtain, wash it regularly to prevent mould.
- Clean the walls with an anti-mould cleaner if they start to show signs of mould and condensation.
- Use bin liners in waste bins and empty bins weekly. Clean the bin with antibacterial cleaner or diluted bleach when needed.

What to use

- All-purpose liquid cleaner for walls, floors and tiles.
- Mould remover for grouting and walls.
- Bleach.
- Cleaning cloths.
- Rubber gloves.
- Mop.

Optional

- Anti-bacterial cleaning sprays for walls, toilets and surfaces.
- Cream cleanser.
- Toilet cleaners that remove limescale.

Kitchen

If you want to avoid tummy-upsets then keeping your kitchen clean is vital. Many cases of food poisoning start in the home, so follow a few basic rules of hygiene. There is no need to buy several different products – see oppostite for some cheap ideas.

- Keep work surfaces clean, with hot soapy water, diluted bleach solution or a spray cleaner.
- Have two chopping boards – one for uncooked meat and the other for everything else. Wash both after every use in hot soapy water.
- Wash up as you go.
- Soak very dirty pans or casserole dishes overnight to make cleaning easier.
- Clean the hob on your cooker after every use if there are spills to prevent the build up of food and grease. This makes the job much easier than if you leave it for weeks or months.
- Clean the inside of the oven every couple of months.
- Clear out old food from your fridge weekly.
- Check the use-by dates, but use your common sense too – some foods last longer after these dates. If the food is mouldy, smells or is a very strange colour, it is probably not sensible to keep it. Wipe out the vegetable baskets and throw out old vegetables.
- Clean the inside of your fridge every few weeks. Take everything out, and take the shelves out, wash in hot soapy water, dry and put back. Clean the inside with a solution of bicarbonate of soda and water, as this will not leave your fridge smelling of detergents.
- Defrost the freezer as and when it needs it – usually about twice a year, unless your freezer automatically defrosts. Try to do this when you have only a small amount of frozen food. Wrap up the frozen food in newspaper and put in a cool box to keep it frozen until you can put it back in the freezer. Clean the baskets and put food back that is worth keeping. If any food has defrosted completely, either use it straightaway or discard it.

'If you want to avoid tummy-upsets then keeping your kitchen clean is vital. Many cases of food poisoning start in the home, so follow a few basic rules of hygiene.'

- Clean the sink with a cream cleanser, hot soapy water or a mild bleach solution.

- Change tea towels regularly. Dirty tea towels and dishcloths can harbour more bacteria than toilet bowls. Wash them at 60° and also clean dishcloths in a weak bleach solution overnight.

- Clean waste and pedal bins with mild bleach solution, especially under the lid where old food might be trapped.

- Wash the kitchen floor weekly and either brush up crumbs or vacuum daily.

What to use

- Detergent.

- Bleach.

- Cream cleanser.

- All purpose liquid cleaner for walls, floors and surfaces.

- Oven cleaner.

Optional

- Cleaners for hobs and work surfaces.

- Anti-bacterial cleaners for surfaces.

- Wire wool or soap-filled pads for scouring.

Eco products

There are numerous products that you can use to be environmentally friendly. These tend to be plant-based and do not contain chemicals that are likely to harm the environment. You can buy everything – washing up liquid, floor cleaner, toilet cleaners, washing powders and cloths – to use in the kitchen and most can be found in your local supermarket.

Laundry

To avoid expensive mistakes, follow a few simple rules before anything goes into the machine. If you don't, your favourite jumper could end up several sizes too small or your white T-shirt might come out pale pink!

■ Sort clothes into piles of white and coloured items.

■ Colours can be sorted again into pale colours and dark colours.

■ Check the labels to see what temperature should be used. Most clothes can be safely washed at 40°, but more delicate fabrics might need a 30° wash or even a handwash cycle. Bear in mind the environmental benefits of washing at 30°.

■ Choose the right washing powder or liquid. Non-biological means without enzymes. Enzymes can remove stubborn stains but they can also irritate sensitive skin if the residue is left in the clothes after washing. There are plenty of washing powders and liquids that you can buy which come with or without enzymes. Powders or liquids for coloured clothes have no brighteners and therefore the colours shouldn't fade.

■ Use the right amount of powder or liquid by reading the instructions on the product; too little and the clothes won't be clean, too much and you will waste money.

■ Ensure all pockets are empty – and check for pens, money and tissues!

■ Fasten zips to avoid damage.

■ Bedding, such as sheets and duvet covers, can be washed at 60° to kill off dust mites.

■ Lightly soiled clothes can be washed on a quick wash – usually 30 minutes.

■ Do not over fill the machine as clothes will be very creased and not as clean.

■ Wash denim, such as jeans, on their own for the first couple of washes as they often leak colour. Wash them inside out to prevent colour loss over time.

■ If you tumble dry, be careful; many clothes – especially wool – will shrink. Read the label on the clothes first.

Machine Wash
Different temperatures
may be indicated.

 Ironing
Cool iron.

 Hand Wash

 Ironing
Warm iron.

 Bleaching
A household bleach
(chlorine) may be used.

 Ironing
Hot iron.

 **Bleaching**
A household bleach
(chlorine) must not be used.

 Ironing
Don't iron.

 Drying
Can tumble dry.

 Drycleaning
May be cleaned
in all solvents.

 Drying
Don't tumble dry.

 Drycleaning
Any solvent except
trichloroethylene.

 Drying
Line dry.

 Drycleaning
Petroleum solvent only.

 Drying
Drip dry.
For best results
hang while wet.

 Drycleaning
Must not be drycleaned.

 Drying
Dry flat.

And finally, don't forget...

Halls and landings

If you can, use a doormat at your front and back doors. If your hall gets a lot of wear, think about using a rug on top of the carpet to protect it.

Windows

Clean windows can make a considerable difference to how your home looks. You can buy window cleaning sprays, but you can also use a weak solution of water and household vinegar to wash them, then you can polish them dry with old newspaper.

'Keep the outside of your home clean as well. Ensure that rubbish is put in the dustbins and not left lying open where it will attract vermin.'

If the paint or varnish comes off your window frames, then re-painting can improve the appearance hugely. Preparation is the key; rub down all the old paint, remove any mould and rotten wood, fill with a suitable filler, then paint after you have rubbed the surface smooth. This type of work is best done in summer when the wood has a chance to dry out, and you can leave the windows open while the paint dries.

Outside your home

Keep the outside of your home clean as well. Ensure that rubbish is put in the dustbins and not left lying open where it will attract vermin.

If you want to dispose of old furniture or household items, either take them to a council refuse site or telephone your local council who will usually come and take large items away, although there may be a charge for this.

Summing Up

- Try to do chores regularly rather than an occasional blitz – it's not hard work then!

- Share chores if you share your home.

- Do not buy masses of expensive cleaning products.

- Keep bathrooms and kitchens clean to avoid tummy bugs.

- Use different chopping boards for raw meat and other foods.

- Keep refuse outside securely covered to avoid attracting vermin.

Chapter Seven

Eating Healthily

Living independently will include shopping and cooking for yourself. This will require organisation and budgeting, as well as some basic cooking skills and knowledge of food groups to ensure you stay in the best of health.

What should you eat to be healthy?

The key term here is 'balanced'; no food type has to be completely out of bounds, but equally you should make sure you are getting all the nutrients you need.

Carbohydrates are energy foods such as bread, cereals, potatoes and pulses. They should comprise about one-third (33%) of your diet. Generally speaking, complex carbohydrates such as brown bread or wholewheat pasta provide better quality and longer lasting energy than more refined sugary foods – for example, white bread, white pasta and white rice.

Proteins are made up of amino acids and are key for growth and maintenance of your body. The most abundant source of protein is from meat and fish, but it's also found in dairy products and pulses. Protein from meat, fish, eggs, beans and other non-dairy sources should make up 12% of your diet, and protein from milk and dairy foods should be about 15%.

The rest of your diet should be made up with fruits and vegetables (33%), allowing only 8% for food and drink high in sugar and/or fat.

'The key term here is "balanced"; no food type has to be completely out of bounds, but equally you should make sure you are getting all the nutrients you need.'

The eatwell plate

Use the eatwell plate to help you get the balance right. It shows how much of what you eat should come from each food group.

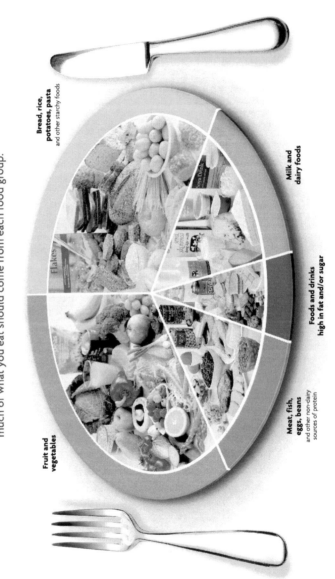

FOOD STANDARDS AGENCY
eatwell.gov.uk

Bread, rice, potatoes, pasta
and other starchy foods

Milk and dairy foods

Foods and drinks high in fat and/or sugar

Meat, fish, eggs, beans
and other non-dairy sources of protein

Fruit and vegetables

Need2Know

Fats and oils are just as essential to your health as any other food group – but some are healthier than others. It is advisable to gain most of the fat in your diet from unsaturated fats, for example omega oils found in fish.

Vitamins and minerals are essential micronutrients which prevent us from becoming sick. Good sources are found in fruit, vegetables, nuts and seeds, which is why it's so important to get your five-a-day.

Fibre is an important component to diet that allows the gut to work properly. Good sources of fibre include:

- Wholemeal, granary and softgrain bread.
- Wholegrain breakfast cereals.
- Wholemeal pasta and brown rice.
- Beans, lentils and peas.
- Vegetables, nuts and seeds.

Government recommendations

How to get your five-a-day

The government recommends you eat five portions of fruit and vegetables a day. Below are some easy ways to include more portions in your diet:

- Breakfast – add fruit such as blueberries, dried fruit and chopped banana to cereals.
- Lunch – add salad to sandwiches and have some pieces of fruit, for example an orange and an apple. You can also use carrot or celery sticks as healthy snacks.
- Dinner – add two or three vegetables to your main meal.
- Fruit juices and smoothies – one glass counts as one portion.
- Swap your usual snack for dried fruit, like raisins or dried apricots.

Two portions of fish per week

Fish contains important omega 3 fats and is a good source of protein. The Food Standards Agency recommends two portions of fish per week, one of which should be oily. Oily fish include: salmon, trout, mackerel, kipper, fresh tuna (not tinned) and anchovies.

For more information about including fish in your diet, go to www.food.gov.uk.

Traffic light meals

'It is healthier to grill meat than to fry it, cutting off any visible fat. Draining the fat off once it's cooked is also a good way to keep meaty meals healthy.'

A simple trick to healthy meals is to try to have a variety of (natural) colours on your plate. For example, red tomatoes, yellow sweetcorn and green salad. Not only will it look good – it will taste good and do you good too!

- Green vegetables contain lots of vitamins and minerals that are good for your health.

- Orange and yellow vegetables contain plenty of vitamin A.

- Pulses, lentils and beans contain a lot of fibre and help to lower cholesterol.

- Potatoes contain lots of vitamin C – eat the skins to benefit from added minerals.

Cooking tips for healthier food

The way we cook our food can have an effect on how healthy something is. You should try to boil vegetables as lightly as possible because over-boiling can sap the nutrients. Instead, leave them 'al dente' to get the most goodness out of them. Steaming is also a good way to lightly cook vegetables.

It is healthier to grill meat than to fry it, cutting off any visible fat. Draining the fat off once it's cooked is also a good way to keep meaty meals healthy.

Fresh, frozen, tinned or dried?

Fruit and vegetables come in many forms, but which is best? Generally speaking, the fresher the food, the more nutritious it is. Frozen vegetables generally keep their vitamin content and dried fruit can be very nutritious, but tinned products can lose much of their vitamins and often there will be a lot of added salt.

Tinned vegetables such as beans, tomatoes and sweetcorn are worth buying, but carrots, peas and potatoes should be bought fresh or frozen if you want to go for the healthy option.

Snacks

Everyone likes to indulge in snacks that have no real nutritional value, but the important thing is to keep snacks like these as special 'treats'. Foods like cakes, biscuits, crisps and pastry are high in calories, sugar and fat.

Eating too much of these types of food can lead to health problems such as high blood pressure, high cholesterol and Type 2 diabetes, which is why a healthy, balanced diet is very important to keeping your body healthy on the inside.

Store cupboard essentials

As well as fresh food, you will need some essentials to make tasty meals. If space is limited, what you buy will have to earn its place. You'll soon get an idea of what you use a lot and what lurks at the back of the cupboard for too long! Here are some suggestions:

- Salt and pepper.
- Olive oil or vegetable oil.
- Ketchup/mayonnaise/soy sauce/sweet chilli sauce.
- Jam and chutney.
- Tea and/or coffee.

- Pasta.

- Rice.

- Pulses such as beans and lentils.

- Plain flour.

- Sugar.

- Tinned food – baked beans, kidney beans, chick peas, tuna, tomatoes, sweetcorn.

- Herbs and spices – you can make homemade curries using different spices, much cheaper than a jar of curry sauce.

- Frozen products – frozen peas, beans, sweetcorn, chips, fish, meat.

For quick and healthy recipe ideas, see *Student Cookbook: Healthy Eating – The Essential Guide* (Need2Know).

Storing food

- Storing food at the right temperature is important to preserve its life and to prevent food poisoning. You should read the labels and follow the manufacturer's advice. All foodstuffs will come with a use-by date, but use your common sense – and if something smells or looks unusual, err on the side of caution. On the flip side, use-by dates can sometimes be over-cautious, so it's advisable to use common sense rather than throw away perfectly edible food. Again, if something looks or smells unusual, it's best not to take the chance.

- It is good to ensure that your fridge is set at the right setting. Usually the highest number on the dial is the coldest, but you may find that food is beginning to freeze if you set it too high. You may need to vary the setting during very hot or cold weather – so keep an eye on this.

- Keep raw meat and fish sealed and away from other foods, especially anything you eat raw, such as fruit or salad.

- Any opened packets or containers of food should be sealed or covered in cling film when in the fridge. Do not store opened cans of food in the fridge; empty the contents into a container, cover and store.

Shopping tips

Food can be very expensive and you will probably find you will have to budget carefully.

How can you eat well and save money?

- Different supermarket chains will vary in their prices, so shop around.

- Check out local markets for cheaper and fresher fruit and vegetables.

- Try out supermarket own brands – sometimes you will find that the packaging is the only difference. However, at other times you will have to pay more for quality.

- Make your meat go further – mince can be bulked out by adding extra vegetables such as carrots, peas and beans.

- If you are cooking for only yourself, it can be economical to split meat packets into freezer bags so you have smaller portions that can be defrosted when needed.

- Buy non-perishable items in bulk. Larger packs of toilet rolls and washing powder often work out more cheaply.

- Look for special offers and reduced items. Find out when most items are reduced – often in the evenings or at weekends. Reduced foods also include those that are close to sell-by date but can be eaten straightaway or frozen.

- Try making double the quantity of meals then freeze one – this saves time, fuel and means you will have a meal ready for when you don't have time to cook.

- Make your packed lunches rather than buying sandwiches. This takes some planning, but it can save you pounds every week. You can make them the night before and keep them in the fridge.

'Try out supermarket own brands – sometimes you will find that the packaging is the only difference. However, at other times you will have to pay more for quality.'

Summing Up

- Have a weekly budget.
- Shop around for the best deals and take advantage of special offers.
- Have a supply of food, either tinned or frozen, for emergencies when you can't shop.
- Buy non-perishable products in bulk or larger packs to save money.
- Try to plan your meals so that you don't resort to buying takeaways.
- Keep your five-a-day in mind and try to eat healthily.
- Store food correctly to avoid deterioration.
- Be aware of use-by dates but also use your own common sense.

Chapter Eight

Looking After Your Emotional Health

Moving away from home for the first time or living independently can be an exhilarating feeling, but it can also be an anxious time. To feel both of these emotions simultaneously is entirely understandable – and normal.

Many young people feel there is an expectation of them to be ecstatically happy when they move out of their parent's home – if you feel homesick or lonely, it can be hard to admit this to your family, friends or even yourself.

Even if you are looking forward to living independently, you might be surprised at how homesick you are. If you are sharing your accommodation then you also have to learn to live with other people who aren't your family – often complete strangers. It would be surprising if it was all plain sailing.

Getting on with your flat mates

If you are sharing a flat or house with strangers, what can you do to ensure you all get on as well as possible?

It is worth remembering that everyone's home environments are completely different. So what was normal for you at home may be very different from other people's experiences and ways of living. If you can treat everyone with consideration, no matter how different they are, it will help. Following some simple rules can make life a lot easier.

- Respect people's possessions – don't borrow anything without asking.
- Don't steal their food, even if you have run out!

'Many young people feel there is an expectation of them to be ecstatically happy when they move out of their parent's home – if you feel homesick or lonely, it can be hard to admit this to your family, friends or even yourself.'

- Keep music to a sensible volume so it won't disturb anyone else.

- Leave the bathroom and kitchen clean and tidy.

- Do not spend hours in the bathroom if it is the only one.

- Respect people's privacy – don't barge into their room without knocking.

- Do ask if it's okay to have friends round, especially if there are lots of them.

- Do ask if it's okay for friends to stay over, particularly if they are going to camp in the lounge.

- Do understand that some people need more sleep – so if you arrive home late, close doors quietly and don't start cooking or playing music if it will disturb anyone else.

- If other people have exams or a stressful time at work, be understanding.

What can you do if other people are inconsiderate?

If you can, tackle any grievances as soon as possible. If you accept their inconsiderate behaviour for weeks, then have an outburst, it will be harder for them to understand why you are suddenly annoyed. Try to talk to them when they are not stressed about something else. When you want to ask someone to change their behaviour, try not to label them or criticise them personally.

For instance, if someone plays music late at night, don't say, 'You are really inconsiderate and selfish', but tell them how it makes you feel. Use 'I' – for example: 'I found it hard to sleep last night. I don't know if you realise how loud the music sounds from my room.' This gives them the opportunity to see it from your point of view and you aren't labelling them. Try not to be confrontational, or shout, as this rarely works and the argument will simply escalate.

Talking it over

If you are sharing a house where everyone comes and goes at different times and there is never the opportunity to talk about anything, it might help to arrange a time when you can all talk. Once a month or so, you could all agree on a time when you will discuss any grievances, sort out any unpaid bills, discuss arrangements you have made for housework and anything else that needs talking about. This doesn't have to be as formal as it sounds, but it can help deal with issues that might arise – especially if one person is not pulling their weight.

Choosing your flat mates

You may or may not be able to choose your flat mates. If you are a student going to university, the likelihood is that you will be sharing a flat or house with strangers. In the following year though, you may well move into different accommodation, or if you're buying or renting your own property then you might want to find other people to share it. How can you ensure you choose the right people to share with? It's worth considering what type of person you are and what kind of friends you have or want. Ask yourself the questions below:

- Are you the life and soul of the party?

- Are you a quiet and studious person?

- Do you want to be friends with your flat mates – or just need someone to pay the rent and keep a low profile?

- Do you want a mix of male and female?

- Are you a neat and tidy person or more laid-back about housework?

If you are looking for sharers, it is best for everyone to be very honest at the start. Make a list of questions you want to ask. No matter how much you might like the potential sharer, if they have a totally different lifestyle, interests or friends, it may simply not work. If they drink a lot, take drugs or smoke and you don't, then think seriously about how you could live with that.

Disagreements in shared houses often result from issues such as these:

- Different lifestyles, including making a lot of noise and coming in late at night.

- Differing standards of cleanliness and tidiness.

- Not paying bills or rent on time – or not having the money to do so.

- Inviting lots of friends around when others might want some quiet time.
- Using other people's food without asking and not replacing it.
- Borrowing other people's possessions without asking.
- Being irresponsible about safety and security.
- Not doing a fair share of the chores.

To make it an easier experience, you can establish your ground rules and be open with anyone who wants to share with you. If you have other friends or acquaintances who know the potential sharers, ask around for their opinions. It is better to take longer to find the right person than to make a mistake.

Sharing your own home

If you're buying your home, or even if you're renting it but want to share the cost with someone, you need to think about this carefully.

- Is this purely a business arrangement? Or are you looking for a friend as well?
- How will you feel about another person using your possessions?
- How much privacy do you want? Could this change?
- Are you allowing them to share the whole house, or just their room, kitchen and bathroom?
- Are you sure they are trustworthy and able to look after your home if you are away?
- If you're renting, your lease may not allow you to sub-let even if you are the main leaseholder. You should check it before making any arrangements for a lodger.

Feeling homesick

It is normal to miss your friends, family, pets and familiar surroundings. No matter how eager you are to be independent, the reality may be different. If you can expect to feel slightly homesick at times, it can be easier to cope with than if you expect to settle in immediately. Try to believe that you will feel more at home eventually, and that everyone else probably feels like you do to an extent.

People with homesickness may describe their feelings as sadness, depression, hopelessness and frustration. The most effective ways of coping include keeping a positive attitude, having regular contact with home and being active in your new environment.

What can you do to feel more settled?

Everyone is afraid of rejection to some extent, but if you are starting university, remember that everyone is in the same boat. If you move to a new area for a reason other than starting university, some of the following ideas may also be of use.

- Join some clubs. Even if you aren't too sure about whether they are for you, give them a go. Don't give up after a week – it can take a few weeks until you get to know other people.

- Instead of looking for friends, try being a friend. Talk to other people who seem quiet or possibly lonely.

- Share a meal you are cooking or offer to help someone with something.

- Keep in touch with your family and friends from home, but not too much.

- Don't be afraid to tell people if you are homesick; they may be too.

- Try not to go back to your family home too often – such as every weekend – as it will make it harder to settle.

- Give yourself time to adjust. Even if you feel very homesick, do not consider going back home until you have given your new home a good two or three months. By this time, you might have developed friendships and feel more settled.

If you have really serious problems with adjusting to your new way of life, consider talking to someone professional; there are many support systems in place at universities or through your GP. If you become very lonely, don't forget the Samaritans offer a 24-hour helpline (see help list for details).

Ways to build your confidence and self-esteem

It is easy to assume that everyone who seems very confident genuinely is and always has been. Not so. Very few people are born with bags of self-confidence; it is something that is learned. This is not the same as appearing insincere, which others will pick up, but about making changes to your thinking and behaviour.

- Make a list of your good points. This can be anything from making a great curry or playing an instrument, to being a loyal friend or a good listener.

- Choose one of these and write it on a post-it where you can see it. Change it every week to something different.

- Keep a record of your personal achievements. If you do something positive every day, no matter how small, note it down. Read these when you are feeling down or needing a boost.

- Push your boundaries. Set yourself an achievable goal, such as talking to one new person each day, or going somewhere new on your own for the first time.

- Make the best of yourself. If you think you would feel more confident with a different hairstyle or different clothes, do it.

- Learn to act confidently. If you think confidently then your actions will follow. Reflect on how a confident person behaves. Do they smile a lot? Make eye contact? Have open body language? If you copy this, you will feel more confident.

- Stop believing that everyone is better than you are. Everyone is a mixture of strengths and weaknesses.

- Think positively. If you can believe in a positive outcome, it is more likely to happen than if you think negatively.

- Change your negative thoughts to positive ones by eradicating the words such as can't, won't and don't from your thoughts and substituting with can, will and do.

Are you depressed?

Depression is an illness that can affect anyone in varying degrees. If you feel very down and have some of the following symptoms, it would be sensible to see your GP.

- Sadness or hopelessness.
- Irritability, anger or hostility.
- Tearfulness or frequent crying.
- Withdrawal from friends and family.
- Loss of interest in activities.
- Changes in eating and sleeping habits.
- Restlessness and agitation.
- Feelings of worthlessness and guilt.
- Lack of enthusiasm and motivation.
- Fatigue or lack of energy.
- Difficulty concentrating.
- Thoughts of death or suicide.

'If you feel down but don't think that you are seriously depressed or need to see a GP, try exercise which releases endorphins that make you feel good.'

But do remember that not everyone who has these symptoms is depressed; you know what is normal for you. On the flip side, this is not an exhaustive list of symptoms of depression, nor is it a self-diagnosis tool. If you feel that your homesickness is more serious than simply feeling down now and again, seek help. Should you be concerned about any of your friends who exhibit these signs, try to persuade them to get help.

If you suffer from depression, seeing your GP will mean you receive the right treatment. This can be drugs or counselling, or a combination.

Exercise has been shown to help depression. If you feel down but don't think that you are seriously depressed or need to see a GP, try exercise which releases endorphins that make you feel good.

A regular daily visit to the gym, a run or a walk might be all you need to make you feel better. Remember too that any abuse of anything mood-altering, from drugs to too much caffeine and alcohol, can exacerbate feelings of depression. For more information on depression, see *Depression – The Essential Guide* (Need2Know).

Being able to say no

When you first leave home, you will be with an entirely new set of people; they may have different values to you and behave differently to what you are familiar with. Sometimes you might feel pressurised into behaving in ways that you are not comfortable with, in order to be part of the crowd. You will want to be accepted and liked, but that doesn't mean you have to participate in anything that you're not comfortable with.

There is a culture, particularly at university, for drinking a lot. Some people find it hard to resist, going with the crowd rather than making a stand. Try to make friends with people like yourself; these may not be the first people you meet, but you will find others. Don't be pressurised into doing anything you're uncomfortable or uneasy about.

Summing Up

- Accept it can take a few weeks or longer to settle in somewhere new.

- Make the effort to meet new people.

- Be considerate to other people in your accommodation.

- Tackle any problems with people in your house sooner rather than later.

- If you feel homesick, share your thoughts with other people around you.

- Do not isolate yourself if you are unhappy – tell your friends or family.

- Seek help from your GP if you feel very down and this feeling doesn't go away.

- Don't feel you have to deal with feelings of depression or homesickness on your own. If there is no one you can talk to, the Samaritans are available anytime.

- Don't allow new friends to pressurise you into taking part in an activity you're uncomfortable with.

Chapter Nine

Looking After Your Physical Health

When you live independently for the first time, you have to be able to look after every aspect of your health – emotional and physical.

GPs

If you are at university, it is likely that you will be asked to register with a GP's surgery. This registration is usually done during the first week or two. It is important that you do this – if you are ill, it can be harder to get immediate treatment if you are not registered. If you ever need a home visit then you will need to be registered first.

If you are not at university, you will have to find a GP's surgery which will accept you. Your surgery may be the only one in your town, or you might have a choice. Recommendations are always good, so ask neighbours and friends.

'When you start university and are living in accommodation with lots of other people, you are likely to come across freshers' flu.'

Dentists

Similarly, you might want to register with a dentist, unless you are going to stay with one near your previous home. Dentists are either NHS or private. If you can only find a private dentist then ask about their costs for treatment, as all dentists are different. Unlike GPs, your dentist does not have to be within a certain distance of your home – you can see any dentist anywhere but most GP practices operate a catchment area system to ensure home visits can be carried out.

If you feel ill

When you are looking after yourself, one of the hardest decisions is when to see a GP and when to just wait for your illness to go. Without the reassuring influence of your parents, this can sometimes be difficult.

When you start university and are living in accommodation with lots of other people, you are likely to come across freshers' flu and/or meningitis at some point. Freshers' flu is common and not too serious, but meningitis can be fatal. It can be hard to distinguish between the two, so get help if you have any doubts. Below is an overview of the two.

Freshers' flu

This is the generic name for a viral infection that is often transmitted during freshers' week. Putting hundreds of young people together who have not had much sleep but often plenty of alcohol, and with strains of viruses to which they have little immunity, and it suddenly becomes easy to get ill.

Freshers' flu symptoms may include:

- A temperature.
- A sore throat.
- Sneezing.
- Headache.
- Sweating or shivering, or both.
- A cough.

Viral infections cannot be treated with antibiotics, unless you develop a chest or throat infection as well. The best you can do is stay warm, in bed if you feel really unwell, keep away from other people, drink plenty of fluids, take paracetamol and wait for it to pass. If you develop a hacking cough with phlegm or a very sore throat and it is hard to swallow, see your GP in case you have a secondary infection. Please see www.nhs.uk for more information on treatments of flu and common colds.

Meningitis

There are two kinds of meningitis – viral and bacterial. Bacterial meningitis is the most severe. If you have a combination of any of these symptoms below, you must get medical help immediately – go to hospital or dial 999. Do not delay.

- A rash that doesn't fade under pressure (try pressing a glass against the skin).
- High fever.
- Severe headache.
- Stiff neck.
- Dislike of bright light.
- Drowsiness.
- Confusion and irritability.
- Vomiting.
- Muscle pains.
- Cold and pale hands and feet.
- Diarrhoea.

If you spot any of these symptoms in your friends, make sure that you get medical help. It can be hard to be certain what is wrong, especially if the person is drowsy and in bed. However, it is better to have a false alarm than to take the risk of not getting help.

Being responsible with alcohol

Drinking and getting drunk is very common and almost a rite of passage for many young people beginning university or socialising outside of work with other young people. You might feel pressurised into drinking more than you want to, especially if you are living with people who drink a lot. However, it might be helpful to look at a few statistics about alcohol, so you know what the safe limits are.

Intake of alcohol is measured in units; a unit is classed as 10ml of alcohol. It's important to remember that one drink does not equal one unit – it depends on the strength and the quantity. For example, a 330ml bottle of medium 4% strength beer will have around 1.3 units, and a small glass of wine with an alcohol volume of 12% will be 1.5 units.

On a daily basis, men should not drink more than 3-4 units, and women 2-3. It is recommended that everyone has at least one alcohol-free day a week. There is a useful unit calculator that can be found at www.units.nhs.uk/questions/unit-calculator.

What are the dangers of drinking too much?

'On a daily basis, men should not drink more than 3-4 units, and women 2-3. It is recommended that everyone has at least one alcohol-free day a week.'

On a day-to-day basis, drinking too much can be detrimental to your body and your emotional health. Alcohol can deplete your body of vitamins and minerals, and cause dehydration which will affect your skin. If you are moderately drunk, you may behave in ways that are out of character for you and make decisions which put your personal safety at risk, or that you find embarrassing later on. Longer-term dangers of too much alcohol over a long period are:

- Cancer of the mouth and throat, and breast cancer in women.

- Heart disease and stroke.

- Liver disease, including cirrhosis and liver cancer.

- Depression, especially if you are already suffering from homesickness or symptoms of depression.

From a financial perspective, buying a lot of alcohol is expensive. If you are budgeting for the first time, you can easily overspend by drinking too much and too regularly.

Binge drinking is defined as drinking five or more drinks over a short amount of time. Sometimes people think that drinking a large amount of alcohol relatively infrequently is safer than drinking regularly. This is not the case, if you binge drink, you are still at risk from all the dangers of longer-term drinking.

If you have a friend who shows any of these signs, get medical help:

- They are unconscious and cannot be woken.

- Their breathing is shallow.

- They feel cold.

If you're in any doubt about someone displaying these signs, the advice is to call 999. Try to keep them sitting up to prevent them choking on their own vomit and give them some water if they can take it. If they're passed out, lay them in the recovery position and check their breathing. Keep the person warm until the emergency services arrive.

There are some actions you should not take if a friend is showing signs of alcohol poisoning. Do not make them drink coffee as it will dehydrate them even more, and it's not a good idea to make them walk around or put them under a cold shower.

How can you enjoy yourself and be responsible with alcohol?

Make sure you don't drink on an empty stomach as food helps to absorb alcohol. Try to keep a count of how much you are drinking and know the strength of the drinks – beer and wine can vary hugely. Another idea is to alternate your drinks with water or soft drinks; tap water is available for free in most pubs and clubs. Don't be persuaded to drink more than you feel comfortable with, and organised pub crawls should be avoided, or at least only indulged in once in a while!

Know what is in your drink

If you are drinking in a pub or club, make sure that you buy your drinks or have a trusted friend buy them. A few tips to keep safe while out in pubs and clubs are:

- Don't leave your drink unattended.

- Don't accept drinks from people you do not know.

- Keep an eye on your friends' drinks.

- If you are in a situation where you feel uncomfortable, leave.

Close relationships

Beginning university or becoming independent from your family will inevitably give you more freedom; this may mean becoming more sexually active or becoming more sexually active than before. This is a natural reaction to your new found independence, but you should always make sure you use protection against sexually transmitted infections (STIs) and pregnancy.

Contraception

There are many methods of contraception. The two most commonly used are the combined pill and condoms. Condoms will protect you against STIs and pregnancy – so, as a female, if you are taking the pill, using a condom is also necessary.

'Condoms will protect you against STIs and pregnancy – so, as a female, if you are taking the pill, using a condom as well is necessary.'

Methods of contraception

Hormonal methods of contraception provide the best protection against pregnancy, but they don't protect against sexual infections. STIs can only be protected against by using barrier methods like condoms.

- The combined pill – if taken correctly, it's almost 100% effective. If you have a tummy upset, including diarrhoea, or take certain antibiotics, you need to be aware that its effectiveness can be reduced.

- The progesterone-only pill, or mini-pill, is less effective and is prescribed mainly for women for whom the combined pill is not suitable.

- Condoms are the only contraceptive to prevent pregnancy and STIs. When used correctly, they're 98% effective. But you must make sure they are not ripped or out of date.

- The IUD (inter uterine device) and IUS (inter uterine system) are small devices made of copper or plastic, positioned inside the uterus. They do not prevent conception but work by preventing implantation. The IUS is coated with the hormone progesterone which is gradually released. It can now be prescribed for heavy periods as well as a contraceptive. Both the IUD and the IUS are effective – over 99%.

- Hormonal implants and injections are very effective. However, implants have the disadvantage that they need removal if you have side effects, and injected hormones cannot be reversed.

- Diaphragms can be effective up to around 98% if used correctly, but they are perhaps not the first choice if you really want the best protection possible.

- The morning after pill can be safely taken as an emergency contraceptive up to 72 hours after sex. It is not 100% effective so if you are having regular sex, you need another method.

The combined pill is the most popular and effective method, unless you cannot take it for any reason. If this is the case, your GP or family planning centre will discuss other options. Remember that any contraceptive needs to be used correctly and regularly to be effective. If you take a risk with pregnancy, you might also be taking a risk with STIs.

Whether you're male or female, remember that condoms help protect against STIs. For more information see *Sexually Transmitted Infections – The Essential Guide* (Need2Know) and *The Pill – An Essential Guide* (Need2Know).

Abortion

An abortion should not be viewed as a type of contraception – but if contraception fails, it may be an option. In 2008 there were around 195,000 abortions in the UK. The largest percentage of abortions performed, almost 4 in 100, were on women aged 19.

If you think you want an abortion, consult your GP or family planning clinic as soon as you can. There are also private clinics, such as the Brook Centres, who will see anyone aged under 25, or the British Pregnancy Advisory Service – BPAS. The earlier the abortion is carried out, the easier it is for your emotional and physical health. Even if you are unsure about an abortion, the doctor can put you on the waiting list, which can be two to four weeks, whilst you decide.

Abortions are either medical or surgical. Up to nine weeks, pregnancy can be terminated by drugs – taking oral tablets. Up to 15 weeks, the abortion can be done using vacuum aspiration via the vagina. Beyond 15 weeks the method used will depend on various factors which will be discussed with you.

'Condoms are the only contraceptive to prevent pregnancy and STIs. When used correctly, they're 98% effective. But make sure they are not ripped or out of date.'

If you choose to have an abortion, you will need emotional support. The centres that provide abortions also offer this, but you may want to involve your close friends and family as well. For more information, please see *Abortion – The Essential Guide* (Need2Know).

Sexually transmitted infections

STIs don't just happen to other people – or people who have numerous partners. Anyone who has had sex – or whose partner has – can be at risk. You can carry infections and be symptom-free. This is how many infections are spread; the initial symptoms may be short-lived or vague, so the person who is infected doesn't realise. They then unknowingly infect another person. This sequence is repeated and the infection rapidly spreads. There are many different infections, some of which can cause infertility and more serious health problems.

'In the UK in 2008 there were an estimated 123,000 cases of chlamydia, according to NHS statistics.'

Chlamydia

One of the most common infections is chlamydia. It has been estimated that up to 10% of women under the age of 25 are infected – and as many as 75% do not know they are infected. In the UK in 2008 there were an estimated 123,000 cases of chlamydia, according to NHS statistics.

Chlamydia can be transmitted by oral, genital or anal sex. However, between 70-80% of women have no symptoms, and neither do 50% of men. If symptoms occur, they are similar in women and men. These can include an abnormal discharge and a burning pain on urinating. In women, further symptoms when the infection has spread from the cervix to the uterus or fallopian tubes can include fever, abdominal pain, pain during sex and bleeding between periods. Chlamydia can lower fertility in men and women.

If you have unprotected sex with anyone – and that is sex without a condom – then you should be tested for chlamydia, whether you or they have symptoms or not. Treatment is easy if caught early and involves antibiotics. You can get a free test kit in most areas by post, if you are under 25, by contacting the British Pregnancy Advisory Service. You can also buy test kits from Boots for around £25, or the kit is free if you live in London and are under 25.

Gonorrhoea

Gonorrhea is common, with over 16,000 cases annually. Like chlamydia, it can be caught through genital, anal and oral sex. The symptoms are very similar to chlamydia, but sometimes they do not appear for up to a month afterwards – by which time anyone carrying it could have infected others.

Longer-term, untreated gonorrhoea can be serious. In both men and women it can cause infertility, and further complications can include arthritis, heart conditions and eye infections. If left untreated, it can be life threatening. Treatment is with appropriate antibiotics, so if you have any symptoms at all after sexual contact, make sure you are checked out.

Genital herpes

Genital herpes is transmitted by the herpes simplex virus which causes cold sores. It is characterised by small blisters on the genitals which burst and then leave the skin feeling sore and tender. The skin can take two to four weeks to heal, and secondary outbreaks can occur at any time.

The treatment is with anti-viral drugs, but none can cure the virus completely. The only way to avoid infection is to not have sex with anyone who has the virus, or is being tested for it. Other than that, which can be hard to know, use a condom. This will not give 100% protection, as the skin that is not covered could be carrying the virus.

'If you think that you have an STI – or are simply worried about some symptoms – then get help, sooner rather than later.'

Genital warts

Warts are caused by the human papilloma virus – HPV. Infection with this virus is common but not all people will show symptoms.

Warts may be visible, but they might also be found in the vagina and on the cervix. Left untreated, warts can contribute to changes in the cervix and are now implicated in the development of cervical cancer. Men can also be at risk from penile cancer.

If you have genital warts, get treatment. This can include liquids which kill the warts, or they might be frozen off. If you are a woman and have had genital warts, then you should have more frequent cervical smears as the wart virus raises your risk of cervical cancer. Again, not having multiple partners, not smoking, and having safe sex will help you avoid contracting the warts – but condoms do not provide 100% protection.

Syphilis

Syphilis can be a very serious infection if left untreated. It can be fatal, though not until 10 or 20 years after infection has occurred.

The first sign is a painless sore or ulcer, and you might also have a fever, tiredness and enlargement of lymph nodes. Transmission is through sex – vaginal, anal or oral – with an infected person who has an ulcer. If you are infected, the sore will appear anywhere between 10 days and three months after infection.

Treatment is relatively easy with antibiotics. Avoidance of the disease means not having sex with anyone whose sexual history you do not know or who will not be open about their sexual history. Condoms can reduce the risk but not eliminate it completely.

Hepatitis A, B, C and HIV/AIDS

With the exception of hepatitis A, these serious diseases are spread by sexual contact and also by blood. You are at risk if you have sex with anyone who is infected and if you take drugs that involve needle-sharing.

All these infections affect your whole body and all can be fatal, except hepatitis A which usually clears up in a few months. If you feel unwell and think you could have put yourself at risk from any of these diseases, you must seek medical help.

Other infections

Thrush

Many women get thrush which is a yeast infection that can be passed on to men and then back to their partners. It can be caused when the bacterial balance of the body is changed, for example by taking antibiotics. Thrush causes irritation of the vulva and penis. In women there is usually a creamy discharge, intense itching and possibly tiny red spots. In men there may be a rash on the penis and possibly a discharge.

Treatment is with creams, pessaries or oral drugs. If either partner has thrush, it is important that both partners are treated otherwise reinfection is possible.

Lice and mites

These are not necessarily transmitted sexually – but they can be. Lice can live in pubic hair and cause intense irritation. Mites, such as scabies, live in the folds of the skin, including the genitals and hands. Whilst neither of these is life threatening, they are not pleasant to live with and should be treated. Treatment is relatively easy with lotions.

Where to get help

If you think that you have an STI – or are simply worried about some symptoms – then get help, sooner rather than later.

You can either go to your doctor or, if you prefer, a genitourinary clinic – GU clinic. You can find the details of your nearest one in the telephone directory or online – go to www.nhs.uk and click on 'find and choose services', then 'sexual health'.

BPAS provides free postal test kits for chlamydia in most areas and can also test for some other infections by post.

GU clinics will treat you in confidence. Although you might feel embarrassed, be assured that the staff will do their utmost to put you at your ease. Your behaviour will not be judged; their role is to treat you. Treatment is free and sometimes they have a 'walk-in' system, so you do not need to make appointments. They may have separate women's and men's clinics so you will not bump into anyone you could be embarrassed to see.

Getting treatment for an STI is essential. It goes without saying that until you have been treated, you should not have sex with anyone. It is also sensible not to have sex if you even suspect you have an infection. If you have caught an infection, it is responsible to tell your partner, or ex-partner, that they could be infected, so that the cycle of infection can be controlled.

Summing Up

- Register with a doctor and dentist as soon as possible.

- Take symptoms that could be meningitis very seriously – for yourself and your friends.

- Be aware of how much you are drinking within health guidelines.

- Remember that being drunk can result in irresponsible behavior and put you at risk in various social situations.

- If you are sexually active, be responsible for contraception.

- If you have unprotected sex, or suspect your new partner has had unprotected sex, get checked out confidentially at a GU clinic.

- If you have an STI, complete the treatment and inform any partners who may need treatment.

Chapter Ten

Getting Ready to Buy Your Home

So, you want to buy your own home. What do you need to know before you start?

First – have you done the financial calculations? If you have been sharing a home, you will have shared your outgoings. If you buy, you will be responsible for all the bills and upkeep, as well as the mortgage. These bills will include utility bills, telephone, council tax, water rates, house insurance – buildings and contents – and possibly annual maintenance charges if you live in a block of flats.

The differences between renting and buying are mainly around commitment and costs. It doesn't cost anything to end your tenancy and move. If you buy, then want to move, you will have to fund the sale of your home. In addition, you risk being in a negative equity situation if house prices fall: this is when the house is worth less than you bought it for, so you cannot clear your mortgage with the sale alone.

The costs involved in buying or selling a home include:

- Stamp duty.
- Estate agents' fees.
- Home Information Pack – HIP.
- Mortgage arrangement fees.
- Survey.

'The differences between renting and buying are mainly around commitment and costs. It doesn't cost anything to end your tenancy and move. If you buy, then want to move, you will have to fund the sale of your home.'

- Solicitor's fees.

Stamp duty is a tax paid to the government. Currently this is 1% of the value of your home between £125,000 to £250,000, with a minimum payment of £1,250. To keep up-to-date with any changes, visit www.direct.gov.uk.

Estate agents' fees are paid by the vendor – the seller. These vary depending on whether you instruct a single agency or use multiple agents. The fee is around 1-2.5%.

A HIP is currently required from the seller. It gives you information about the property, including the energy performance of the home, as well as details of searches.

Mortgage arrangement fees are a fee levied by your mortgage provider. They vary but are usually around £200-300. Some lenders will provide mortgages without this fee – shop around.

A survey will be required by the mortgage provider. They will carry out their own basic survey, but if the property is old or there is some query over structure, then you will usually have to pay a higher fee for a more in-depth survey.

Solicitor's fees are paid for the solicitor to handle the sale. This involves them drawing up the contract between you, the buyer, and the vendor. They will handle the legal aspects of the sale to exchange of contract and completion (when the keys are handed over and the property is yours).

Raising the capital

How do you obtain a mortgage?

First, accept that you need to shop around. There are numerous banks and building societies that will offer to lend you money, but the repayments and deals vary enormously. Sometimes it can be favourable to borrow from a building society you already have a savings account with, as they look on you as a current customer. This might make it easier to obtain the mortgage, especially if you save regularly and have no outstanding debts.

It is a good idea to make appointments with several banks or building societies to find out which of them can offer you the best deal. Also look online for details of their current offers and make a short-list of lenders who appear to offer what you need. Some lenders offer an online facility where you can enter your salary, the length of term of your mortgage and the deposit you have. Using this information it can calculate how much you can borrow and how much monthly repayments would be.

How much can you borrow?

This varies, but a rough rule of thumb is three times your annual income. You will be expected to find a deposit of between 10-25%. So, if the property costs £100,000, you could possibly borrow £75,000 – maybe more with a smaller deposit – based on your annual income of £25,000. If you are buying with another person, so you become joint owners, then it is unlikely you can borrow three times your joint income. Following the 'credit crunch', lenders have become much more wary of allowing customers to borrow huge amounts. You also have to consider job security for both parties, as well as longer-term job prospects.

Take your time deciding which mortgage is best for you. Many lenders offer fixed rate mortgages. This means the interest rates are fixed for a period of time, such as two or three years, at a rate lower than other interest rates. The benefit of this is that you are protected from interest rate rises, but the disadvantage is that if interest rates fall, you will not benefit.

You also need to consider what happens when you come to the end of the fixed term; can you afford higher rate payments? It is tempting to choose a fixed rate mortgage when you are getting onto the housing ladder, but it is worth considering the overall trend of the money market; if a fall in interest rates is predicted, then a fixed rate is not so attractive.

You may find it useful to see an independent mortgage adviser – your estate agents may be able to put you in touch with one, or you could ask other fellow home-owners for advice.

'You will be expected to find a deposit of between 10-25%.'

Mortgage indemnity

If you want to borrow a larger sum than 75% of the property value, you may be able to, but at a higher cost. In order to protect themselves from defaulted repayments, the lender may take out insurance on the loan – mortgage indemnity. This cost is not passed on to you directly, but you may well find that the only mortgage offers you have are at a higher interest rate, in order to offset the lender's additional costs.

Changing your mortgage provider

'Don't forget to look at properties that are slightly more expensive than you can afford, as everyone expects you to make an offer below the asking price.'

Take as much time as possible to ensure you choose the best deal. It is possible to change mortgage providers later – and indeed you should actively do so if you can get a better deal. However, there are often financial penalties for this from your current provider, in the form of a lump sum payment to them.

How soon should you start looking for a property?

It usually takes several months to buy a home, although it can be quicker. When you know that you want to buy, start registering with as many estate agents as you can, and also do your own searches online.

Don't forget to look at properties that are slightly more expensive than you can afford, as everyone expects you to make an offer below the asking price. As a first time buyer, you are in a strong position.

If you have your mortgage arranged and if you buy a new property, then you could move in a matter of weeks, as soon the legal side of it is completed. This makes it more important to have your finances sorted before you see the home of your dreams. You do not want to be 'pipped at the post' by another buyer, just because you have not got your finances in order.

What should you look for when buying?

The main factor is location: is the area sought after? Is it safe? What will the re-sale value of your home be? Can you see it increasing in value?

It is usually better to buy smaller in a good or up-and-coming area than to buy bigger in an area where property will never appreciate in value. Take into account what you might need to spend to update bathrooms and kitchens, or installing new central heating or double-glazing. Also, consider the cost of travel to work, shops and friends.

Don't buy on impulse when you buy your first home. You might be there for many years, so take your time to avoid making expensive mistakes. Once you have made a decision, find the best mortgage, plan your move – and enjoy your first home!

Summing Up

- Find out how much you can borrow and how much the deposit will be.

- Shop around for the best mortgage deals.

- Establish a price range and register with estate agents.

- Expect your house buying to take at least six weeks and possibly much longer.

Help List

Alcoholics Anonymous

PO Box 1, 10 Toft Green, York, YO1 7ND
Tel: 0845 769 7555
www.alcoholics-anonymous.org.uk
Help and support for those affected by alcohol, including their families.

British Association of Removers

www.bar.co.uk
Find removal companies in your area.

British Pregnancy Advisory Centre

Tel: 08475 30 40 30
www.bpas.org
Information on abortion, contraception, STIs and STI testing by post.

Brook Centre

Tel: 0808 802 1234 (helpline, Monday to Friday, 9am-7pm)
www.brook.org.uk
Free confidential advice on contraception, relationships and STIs for the under-25s.

Carbon Monoxide Poisoning

www.nhs.uk/conditions/carbon-monoxide-poisoning
Information on the causes, symptoms, treatment and prevention of carbon monoxide poisoning.

Citizens Advice Bureau

www.citizensadvice.org.uk
Free legal and financial advice. See the website for details of your local branch.

Community Legal Advice

Tel. 0845 345 4 345 (helpline)
www.communitylegaladvice.org.uk
Free legal advice on debt, credit cards, mortgages, housing, renting and repossession.

Family Planning Association

Tel: 0845 122 8690 (England, helpline, Monday to Friday, 9am-6pm)
Tel: 0845 122 8687 (Northern Ireland, helpline, Monday to Friday, 9am-5pm)
www.fpa.org.uk
Free information on contraception, emergency contraception, STIs, pregnancy and abortion.

Food Standards Agency

www.eatwell.gov.uk
Information on eating healthily, food storage, food hygiene and food poisoning.

Freecycle

www.uk.freecycle.org
Freecycle matches people who want to give unwanted items away with those who need them. Search online for items in your area.

Meningitis Research Foundation

Tel. 080 8800 3344 (helpline, Monday to Sunday, 24-hour)
www.meningitis.org
Information and advice on the symptoms and treatment of meningitis.

NHS Alcohol Units Calculator

www.units.nhs.uk/questions/unit-calculator
You can use this units calculator to check if you're drinking within the recommended limits.

NHS Choices

www.nhs.uk

You can find the details of your nearest GU clinic here. Click on 'find and choose services', then 'sexual health'.

Right Move

www.rightmove.co.uk
Website covering the UK, listing properties for sale and for rent.

Samaritans

The Upper Mill, Kingston Road, Ewell, Surrey, KT17 2AF
Tel. 08457 909090 (helpline, Monday to Sunday, 24-hour)
www.samaritans.org
Free helpline for anyone who is unhappy, suicidal, or needs someone to talk to. Email help is also available.

UK Property Shop

www.ukpropertyshop.co.uk
National website of estate agents and properties for sale and to rent in your area.